Where Animals Live

The World of Squirrels

Text by Jennifer Coldrey

Photographs by
Oxford Scientific Films

Gareth Stevens Publishing
Milwaukee

Tree-living Squirrels Around the World

Squirrels may be found in forests like this, as well as in parks and yards, in many countries around the world.

Some squirrels, like this British Red Squirrel, like to live among pine and other *coniferous* trees. →

This North American Grey Squirrel lives among oak and other broad-leaved trees. There are also pygmy and "giant" squirrels in Africa and Asia, and flying squirrels in Asia, Europe, and North America. All of them make the trees their home.

Home in the Trees

Tree-living squirrels come down to the ground to search for food. But their main home is in the trees. There, they are safe from most enemies.

Squirrels build hollow nests, called *dreys*, in the trees. Dreys are made of twigs and bark, and they are lined with moss or grass and dead leaves.

The trees also provide most of the squirrel's food, including nuts, seeds, fruit, buds, and shoots. You can find leftovers from their eating scattered under the trees.

The next time you walk through some trees, look up in the branches. You may see a squirrel climbing and leaping about!

The Squirrel's Body

Tree squirrels are cute animals. They have long and bushy tails, sleek and silky fur, and beady black eyes.

They come in many colors. But greyish brown and brownish red are the most common.

North American Red Squirrels like this one have black lines along their sides in the summer.

↑

European Red Squirrels are found in Britain. They are larger than North American Red Squirrels. They also have long tufts of hair on their ears.

The Grey Squirrel also has tufts of hair on its ears, but only in winter.

← A squirrel's tail is very important. It is used for steering and balancing up in the trees.

← Squirrels have large eyes on the sides of their heads. They give squirrels the good eyesight they need for their high-speed travel through the trees. Squirrels also hear very well and have a good sense of smell.

Squirrels are rodents. This means they have long, sharp front teeth called *incisors*. These teeth are for gnawing and cutting. At the back of the mouth are the grinding teeth, called *molars*.

↓

Squirrels move through the trees like acrobats! They have a good sense of balance. This helps them leap from tree to tree and run along tiny branches.

Squirrels always run down trees head-first. They use their claws to cling to the bark.

Flying squirrels can glide through the air. They have flaps of skin that spread like wings.

Food and Feeding

Squirrels are mainly plant-eaters. Most of their food comes from trees. This squirrel holds a pine cone in its long and slender paws. It is biting off the scales to get at the seeds.

Squirrels use their incisors like a crowbar. This is how they crack open even the hardest nuts.

Here is all that is left of a pine cone after a squirrel has stripped it of its seeds and scales! ➤

Squirrels eat different things at different times of the year. In the autumn, they fatten up on apples, nuts, and other woodland fruits.

In the spring, they eat young buds and other new plants. In the summer, food is harder to find. This is when squirrels eat the bark of young trees. They sometimes eat soil, which contains many minerals and *roughage*. Squirrels rarely drink. They get most of their water from food and dew.

We all know that squirrels bury or hide away nuts and pine cones. This is very helpful for winter and other times when food is hard to find. Squirrels forget about many of the nuts and cones they bury. These often sprout and grow into trees!

13

Activities

Tree squirrels are very active in the early morning and late afternoon. On warm summer days, they love to lie on the branches in the sun.

In cold, wintry weather, squirrels spend lots of time sleeping in their nests.

↑

In winter, squirrels come out in the middle of the day to look for food. They cannot live for more than a few days without food. This is why squirrels do not *hibernate* during the winter.

Sometimes, in winter, squirrels live together in the same drey or nesting hole. But most adult squirrels live on their own.

Behavior

Each squirrel has its own *territory,* and it even marks it with its scent. But squirrels do not guard their home areas very carefully. Sometimes the territories even overlap.

Squirrels are clean animals. They wash themselves often. This keeps their skin and fur free from ticks and other *parasites.*

Squirrels often chase each other and fight playfully.

They show their feelings in many ways. They flick their tails, stamp their feet, and make different noises.

Squirrels are nervous and have very good senses. They are always on the alert and often sniff the air for danger.

Starting a Family

Some squirrels have babies once a year. Others have them twice a year, in early spring and mid-summer.

During courtship, many males chase one female. She mates with the first male to reach her.

Once pregnant, the female makes a soft, warm nest for her family.

↑

The baby squirrels are born six weeks after mating. They are pink and hairless, and their eyes and ears are closed. They cannot hear or see, and each one weighs only ½ ounce. They are only 4 inches long — including their tails!

Fathers are not allowed in the nest, and they do not help raise the babies.

Growing Up

The mother keeps the babies warm and feeds them milk. She must also protect them. If danger threatens, she will move them to a new drey.

When the babies are four or five weeks old, they are covered with fur. And now, their eyes and ears have just opened. They will not be fully *weaned* until they are ten weeks old.

These young squirrels are having fun exploring a bird house! At four months, they will be able to build their own homes. They will be fully grown by seven months, and they will be able to breed before they are one year old.

Natural Enemies and Ways of Escape

Few *predators* can harm squirrels up in the trees. Sometimes, however, birds of *prey* catch them.

Animals like martens and weasels can climb trees and attack young squirrels in the nest.

Squirrels are in much more danger on the ground. There, they are hunted by snakes, birds, foxes, and dogs.

On the ground, squirrels must use their sharp senses to avoid danger. If they remain very still, their color will help hide them.

Humans and Other Dangers

Humans kill squirrels, too. Some, like this gamekeeper, hunt or trap squirrels to protect trees that squirrels damage.

People also harm squirrels by cutting down large numbers of trees. This takes away their home and destroys their woodland *habitat.*

In some places, people hunt squirrels for sport and to provide fur or even food.

Squirrels die from other causes, too. Harsh winters kill many, and some die from forest fires and other accidents.

Squirrels as Pests

Squirrels can do a lot of damage to trees. In the spring, they eat the young buds and branches off of trees. They also peel bark off of trees to get at the sweet sap beneath. If they peel off a whole ring of bark, the tree may die.

Squirrels can also be pests in people's yards, fields, and orchards. There, they eat crops and sometimes damage trees. Some squirrels, like this Grey Squirrel, are so bold that they will steal food from bird feeders. Some are so tame that they will eat out of people's hands!

Friends and Neighbors

Squirrels share the trees with many animals, mostly birds. One *mammal* that lives in the trees is the dormouse. Unlike squirrels, dormice come out only at night, and they hibernate in winter.

Many birds, like this nuthatch, share the squirrel's taste for nuts. And they, too, are experts at opening them!

Many other mammals live on the forest floor with squirrels. These include ground squirrels and chipmunks, both members of the squirrel family. Chipmunks often scamper up and down trees looking for food.

Life in the Trees

Sometimes different kinds of squirrel live in the same trees. When they live at different levels of the tree, they do not fight over food.

Squirrels form an important link in a food chain. Most of their food comes from the woods. And they, in turn, are eaten by woodland predators.

The Food Chain

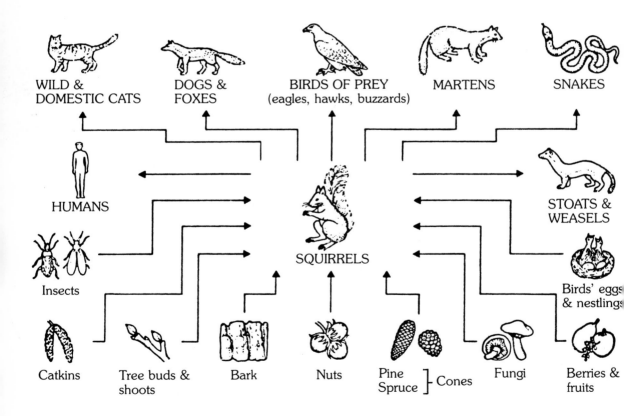

WILD & DOMESTIC CATS

DOGS & FOXES

BIRDS OF PREY (eagles, hawks, buzzards)

MARTENS

SNAKES

HUMANS

Insects

Catkins

Tree buds & shoots

Bark

Nuts

Pine Spruce]- Cones

Fungi

SQUIRRELS

STOATS & WEASELS

Birds' eggs & nestlings

Berries & fruits

Squirrels are perfectly suited for their life in the trees. They are agile and sure-footed. And they manage to find food, shelter, and safety from their enemies. Humans must help them by keeping plenty of forests wild and unspoiled. There, squirrels and other woodland animals will survive.

New Words About Squirrels

These new words about squirrels appear in the text in italics, just as they appear here.

coniferous . . . . cone-bearing (trees) with needle-like leaves, such as pine

dreys . . . . squirrels' nests in the trees, made out of twigs and leaves

habitat . . . . the natural home of any plant or animal

hibernate . . . . to spend the winter asleep

incisors . . . . long, sharp cutting teeth at the front of a squirrel's mouth

mammal . . . . an animal with hair or fur which feeds its young on milk; squirrels, cats, and humans are mammals

molars . . . . back teeth that are used for grinding food

parasites . . . . animals or plants that live and feed on others

predators . . . . animals that kill and eat other animals

prey . . . . an animal that is hunted and killed by another for food

roughage . . . . coarse, indigestible matter in food

territory . . . . piece of land which an animal defends against intruders

weaned . . . . (of young animals) — no longer dependent on their mother's milk for food, but now able to eat other things

Reading level analysis: SPACHE 2.5, FRY 2, FLESCH 91 (*very easy*), RAYGOR 3, FOG 3, SMOG 3.

North American edition first published in 1986 by Gareth Stevens, Inc., 7221 West Green Tree Road, Milwaukee, Wisconsin 53223, USA.

First conceived, designed, and produced by Belitha Press Ltd., London, as *The Squirrel in the Trees,* with an original text copyright by Oxford Scientific Films. Format copyright by Belitha Press Ltd. Typeset by Ries Graphics ltd. Printed in Hong Kong. U.S. Editors: MaryLee Knowlton and Mark J. Sachner. Design: Treld Bicknell. Line Drawings: Lorna Turpin. Scientific Consultants: Gwynne Vevers and David Saintsing.

Library of Congress Cataloging-in-Publication Data

Coldrey, Jennifer.
  The world of squirrels.

  (Where animals live)
  Summary: Describes, in simple text and photographs, the lives of squirrels in their natural habitat explaining how they feed, defend themselves, and breed.
  1. Squirrels — Juvenile literature. [1. Squirrels] I. Oxford Scientific Films. II. Title. III. Series.
  QL737.R68C652   1986   599.32'32   85-30296
  ISBN 1-55532-090-2
  ISBN 1-55532-065-1 (lib. bdg.)

The publishers wish to thank the following for permission to reproduce copyright material: **Oxford Scientific Films Ltd.** for pages 1, 9, 11 *below,* 14 *below* and 16 (photographer G. I. Bernard), pages 3 *above,* 14 *above,* 15, 18, 21, 24, 26 *left* and *right* (photographer John Paling), page 2 (photographer David Thompson), page 5 *left* (photographer G. A. MacLean), pages 3 *below* and 7 (photographer D. J. Saunders), page 11 *above* (photographer Godfrey Merlen), page 12 (photographer Peter O'Toole), page 13 (photographer Dave Houghton), page 25 *below* (photographer Raymond Blythe), page 22 *above,* page 29 (photographer M. P. L. Fogden), pages 16, 23, 28 *above* and 31 (Press-Tige Pictures); British Natural History Pictures for pages 4, 5 *right,* 8, 25 *above* and 28 *below* (photographer John Robinson); Survival Anglia for pages 6 and 10 *left* (photographer Jeff Foott); page 22 *below* (photographer Michael Strobino), and pages 19 and 27 (photographers Liz and Tony Bomford); The Frank Lane Picture Agency for pages 10 *right* and 20 (photographer Steve Maslowski). Front cover photographer: Zig Leszczynski. Back cover photographer: John Paling.